STONY PLAIN

Eli Mandel

PRESS PORCÉPIC

Some of these poems have appeared previously in **Canadian Forum, Made in Canada, 15 Canadian Poets, Ellipse, Fascist Court, Knautical Translations, Waves, Boundary/ 2,** and **Jewish Dialogue.**

The author wishes to thank the Canada Council for assistance during the writing of this book. Evie Mandel first noticed that "Transition Table" could be used as a found poem.

Published by press porcépic, 70 Main St., Erin, Ontario, Canada.

ISBN 0-88878-010-9

By the Same Author

"Minotaur Poems" in **Trio** (1954), **Fuseli Poems** (1960), **Black and Secret Man** (1964), **An Idiot Joy** (1967).

Criticism: The Silent-Speaking Words (1966), **Irving Layton** (1969).

Editor
Five Modern Canadian Poets (1970), **Contexts of Canadian Criticism** (1971), **Poets of Contemporary Canada** (1971), **Eight More Canadian Poets** (1972).

Poetry 62 (1961) with Jean-Guy Pilon.

English Poems of the Twentieth Century (1971) with DES Maxwell.

Table of Contents

STONY PLAIN :

Village 25 miles west of
Edmonton, Alberta

Band of the Assiniboine Tribe,

Reservation south of Lake Wabamun

Estevan, 1934

remembering the family we
called breeds the Roques
their house smelling of urine
my mother's prayers before
the dried fish she cursed
them for their dirtiness their
women I remember too
                        how
seldom they spoke and
they touched one another

even when the sun killed
cattle and rabbis
                        even
in the poisoned slow air
like hunters
                like lizards
they touched   stone
they touched
                        earth

Wabamun

1

lake
    holds
        sun moon stars

10

        trees
           hold

stars moon sun

2

thunder
        and sky
towel
        wet sand
in yellow light

        yesterday

I I

3

on water
many suns
        here there
12   fires then
silent comedians
gulls
perch jumping

4

only
    waves   motion
    sun   dancing

13

no   sun

only
    light
hurting
in its
    endless
dance

5

each day I
step
    farther
into dark water

14

once I will
know
    no longer

whether
        that one
floating
      is myself
or the light
        one
standing
      on the red
pier

6

moon train on causeway

coal cars

15
    a white moon

7

16

to have come to this
simplicity
          to know
only
    the absolute
calm
      lake

    before

    night

8

smell of clover
like sweet stars in a green sky

17   white sweet stars
blossom in a green sky

stars like clover
in a white sky

white
      stars

At Wabamun the Calgary Power Station

leans white in the moon
light puts white slabs up
light shanty whiteness leans

as if it owned the land

daytime horses crop grass
unknowing transformers hum

transformers at the word
it takes on fiery hair
blazing it transmits
messages furious and hairy
it sends and receives from stars
ancient planets   people
who speak like horses new words

then sparks perform dead
parabolas and loops die
fireplace quietens it is
morning it is light only
the power the power hums

and the lake grows green
again in sunlight
                    it is
morning algae and weeds
thicken
            the green lake
wobbles
            we look at
each other   alien forms

Susanna and the Indians

no question she was
tough and probably
frightening like
flash powder/I think
after-images/parents
floating in Jack Chambers'
Messengers Juggling Seed

and that other place wabamun
where an indian woman or
**it could be   a man
eyes bruised   stares**
at streets
            is it
how easily a camera kills
makes me praise poetic sensitivity?

Lake Wabamun: Summer 68

and all the limp, incurious men
my compatriots
                teachers, poets
clerics
        when poems flicker
behind their eyeballs
like the aura epileptics
say they see unbidden
bending like poplars
at the whisper of thunder
rumouring students
rifling private secret files

trouble themselves like wavelets
thrown by a casual craft's
turbulence moving
                small
pebbles only
a savage one dark summer
sifted in idle augury

look a last time
at frogmen and gilas
their webbed hands

reflect
        amphibious
monsters, children
ransack your cities
taught this alien
reckless spasm
neither you nor I
polite summarists
knew poems convulsed

Edmonton, 1967

as if by Colville
I mean "hard edge"
stucco   white wall
gravel &
            legs
in one direction shadows
leaning & midget
above the pavement narrows
rapid as the river
                    everything
disappears
            neatness: axiomatic
            houses   here
now gone
        "You are impatient
with poetry" my friend writes
from Iceland

Oil Refineries: Edmonton

squat
    (are)
and there
                fraction-
ary silver re-
flections   flat
distillation
(silver) in
flat
eye
        pulled side-
-ways a slit in
the mind (&) all

a line   against   some
poem
            not   there

Pastoral

yes as in French films
Gabriel Albicocco's **Le Petit Matin**
how can one forget the beautiful morning

horses plunge through water
remove sweat from your thighs
but believe Germans will come
uniform shining leather rites

how lovely to forget
how luxurious
                we bathe
we atomize ourselves

it is the shampoo
lathers her lathers the horse

and each hazy beautiful morning
ah the Jews trudge wearily
patient meticulous rabbis
their curls their luxurious beards

down between lombardies
between plane trees
elegant tall
                trudge
the Jews each to his
small cabin small crib

lathered
          the Jews
          the Jews

can we not continue with
this business of love

and the aromatic morning
breathing their dead smoke

your eyes gold
I think only of mercy

Two Dog Poems

I

dogs in their boxes
circle before they sleep

in the houses of Calgary
which keep
                    the bare hills
upon which dogs sleep
                                in
their circle of boxes

sometimes I think hills
upon the bare breast of Calgary
excite those milk-white cowboys
                                    who
milk this bursting sky
                            but
the dogs the dogs keep
the great circle of their sleep

2

on the coffee table coloured
comic books but the dogs anyway
run through the pages
                            between
wizards their shining feet

it was the commander's voice
that part in Mozart's play
where the record player goes fuzzy
and between sounds
                        looking
straight at us as if time
stopped the servant girl sang

only
        and I had never noticed
this before she was black

Simulation

we're sorry we cannot
at this time bring
you live
            from
the moon's surface
live transmission

meanwhile we transfer
from the landing area
live to a simulation
of the national medical
programme for
                        healing
cancer

        now you are
looking at a simulated
cancer cell through
a simulated microscope

that dark spot on
the biochemist's cheek
we believe to be a real
live melanoma
                    brought to
you
        in living colour

Reading Room: Periodicals
(also in the annotations of Borges)

seeing he was blind, said: please
clarify systems involved in voice over
and the animation of Walter Cronkite
said in voice over this event is random
do not accept   do not accept
if the seal is broken the unidentified
black object or the unidentified green

and after this looked: a door opened
and a voice said — it was a voice
like Dustin Hoffman's playing Jack
Crabb the oldest man in the world who
really killed Custer said I will give
you a book and in voice over said
do not accept if the seal is broken

and a voice said
                        this is an
autoclock transcript abridged version
this is
            a random event stop clock stop
clock   **there has been a real**
time loss subject has given uncodeable
response
            end
print
        end print
        no change
        programme

                    ends

Two Dream Songs for John Berryman

I

Henry, it says to me here
you took yourself to a bridge.
And you, weary and wavery,
walked, bone and brain, all
to the rail
            there perched
waved farewell from rail

Is that how it was done?

Is it only possible to live
how we have done backwards
dreaming our way from death to
bony life?
            Well, it was gaily
done
      but, here on the coast of Spain,
heartsick like you
                  and hurt too
by burning poems that will not write
themselves I
            say
now fare-you-well
with Sylvia, Ted, Randall,
and all your hurt friends,

God notwithstanding

29

2

It is done but not done well
Henry to betake yourself to ice
and death in a Minnesota morning

30

or a bruise
throwing yourself from bridge
to ice
        why would you want so
to say to me or to God once more
that nothing is fair
among fair women and hardy men

to God
        who never once cared
now name him as you will

it's both night and day
not done well to you or anyone
less or better
                not well

Rembrandt

blunt
      he knew
solidities
        darkness
light
    all those men
    in "The Night Watch"

what it was they saw
in the nooks of their view

but why then
the apostle's style

and why
      the Jewish bride
untouched
      her groom
handling her breast

her lower gown

redder than the darkest ruby?

Snake Charmers
(in memory: A M K)

one, toothless, twirls his gown
around an aroused cobra's eye
another whips his own Medusa head
at an alarmed serpent
                        here
Djemma el Fna, marketplace,
my childhood rises in that charmer's eye,
silks, spices, glittering coins, candied cakes,
all sway before me in this man's vertigo,
his mad mouth frothing at the snake's tongue,
his song, asides to casual drummers and to flutes,
his sideway's step as quirky as the serpent's
lunge, strike like an old flint, an old lamp,
a wick
        Abraham Klein, Irving, Leonard,
you and I could once have sung our songs
here before these snakes, those Arab men
and for these same Jews from Paris or
New York
            Baghdad Teheran Jerusalem
Fez
    tales of the prophet and his magic horse

while wretched blind crippled
through eternal mellahs crawl
Jew upon Jew
                the world's
great serpents
                from that darkness
dazzled
        how

by chance or graceful song

For Jimmy Hendrix and Janis Joplin

it isn't poetry that matters
I'd rather
   there were holes
in this page through which
I could still see you
off at the corner of the TV
lapping the universal crevice

or if not you
at least just to scramble
the syntax and let this
become prose or holes
in the sound I'd call
silence if my own blood stopped
racing
  say
   Gamel Abdul Nasser
I mean the magical
names: the dead motorcyclist
another king of speed and arabia

while my countrymen as
bluff Layton would say
stuff tissues and tampons in
their eyes and noses so they
will not hear
   the hole sound
thing from the
   hole in the room
that goes out into spaced places

the room in 2001
where you hear yourself eat - eaten

the sperm in the eyelid
                              the bone
symphonic and Jimmy's own
organ   mouth
and how Janis you
know your mouth
                    from
a hole in the ground

that emptiness is a sound

your mouth wrapt around mouth
tongue to lip
              to lap
down
      all the whiskey-coloured
nights your staggering cry
where in the dark hole
of his own night Hendrix hung

I loved you Janis
as I love those whom terror seized
for its own poetry: Roethke and Agee
Dylan, Crane, Jarrell, and Sylvia
dead at last in the oven of her own head
not those whom politics silenced or made well
nor the killers on horizons who make guns
their songs and celebrate the will
but drunk, crazed, doped, defeated
by the wild mistake that believes its own art

now Angels will hammer the mob
without shelter we move un
clear into new headlines
our heads in far places
police stating the lanes
staking the hideout's face

35

sexual strings gather
no   vote   the elect
move elsewhere in proud   palaces

space   encloses   closes
the eye
          camera now
the eye is headline
                      you no longer
with us
          we can see through
being   ourselves less visible

only the grain of your uttering
cries
       where there might have been

       black planets

       white dwarves

the harvesters sharpen their knives

Feedback

```
feedback
 feedbackeedback
  feedbafckedback
   feedbaeckdback
    feedbeackback
     feedeadbkack
      fetcelolbodkck
       feecdibaadkk
        feedback  ack
        feedbackackback
        feedbackackbackack
        ack
            backbackack
             backablack
              ackbackk
               bhankk
```

Plaza Mayor

                    because ghosts
will not leave
          my wife
my children
          I play
and replay
the International
Herald Tribune's
           last
report on the Petrosian-Fischer
game for the right to play Spaasky
for the world championship
                and notice
once more all the moves are wrong
at least as the american press tells it

and for that right the young american
his people at war
            wants new air
              light
more money
better hotel rooms

and I'm still cheering for him
for Brooklyn and Forest Hill
against Ukrainia or Bessarabia
or North Moscow
          this place
nervous as a lizard   as if
the cockaded police   the Generalissimo
remembered   the classic square
the king's move   I turn
to **Man's Hope**
          agony
whatever I might choose to say
remains
      abstract
          here
wherever it is that dark comes
ignoring
      families

Desert Words

nothing to say except
Williams' words
to end "The Desert Music"
remember
            "I am a poet! I
am, I am, I am a poet. I
reaffirmed, ashamed"

worth smaller
measure now this voice
time   beside
dying self child
hulks of spain

I am
    I am
            place echoes

lost words
            "sometimes
to record it"

Autobiography

every night I dream I have
wakened to find someone else
has written and published
my autobiography
made of tapes of my own voice
in words I have never spoken

Pioneer 10

when the plaque arrives
male female star and sun
it will be ours
         and
as foretold all
will begin again:
           war
loveliness and
man's desire

when the plaque arrived from outer space, we took it
to the aerospace plant where our astronomers, Sagon
and Drake, were working on the final installation of
the plaque for Pioneer 10 to indicate where our robot
ship had come from and who its builders were — and
compared it with ours: two figures, one male, one
female, an atom, pulsars, a solar system, the robot's
course
       it's ours, they said, and looked again at
the one being installed in the robot, and thought
of Plato's year and turned again to welding nuts and
bolts

Angels in Poems

an old man with heavy wings
in Stevens' poem, in Gabriel Garcia Marquez'
Leaf Storm
               stumbles
now in my poem
                     how else
explain that each day unfolds
like an egyptian calendar

old women in black
no longer gather olives

trees blossom
                  my neighbour's wall
progresses at el capistrano
typico Jaen will be built

do you call that fiction?

angel, you despair
but being merely written
we can say nothing to you

and if it wasn't "measured"?

        much easier I suppose
        to say nothing
                    only
            the programme continues

technically of course
no disaster
            but you know
now your own definition
no longer serves

        Emanations then?

no
    simply presence

later
        all space
collapses messages
return unanswered
or with marks we cannot read

The Death of Don Quixote

ghostly as a line of print
he topples from his bone place
every night a drawn-out passing
death heavy as language
       it is

the cause the word to be
only the word

olive wood burns, almond blossoms
red land of spain and underfoot
path over olive grove grey
slate but on the hilltop red again
as blood is red and iron in the sun's
hot age
    here they burned books
it is why Velasquez learned style
as we know in our own besotted place
Indian towns with French rulers
pretence of elegance and snow
biting at nose and teeth, style

burned into us unlike others
who could kill who could cure
wind sores rude bruise of frost
the dream wired to the dreamer's head
like a space-mask eyes beyond sight

an iron time survival
a style learned in the light
of our own extinction
      "If I have
addressed this incorrectly
will you forgive me?"
       "Penitence?
It is late." Permit me rather
this folly before in iron flame
upon your roadstead burns

not just spain

but all places
   written of

Don Quixote Writes to His Priest

neither their books nor magicians
offer harm to our person or travellers

once a skinned rabbit alarmed us
as did a lamb's head chucked on the road
all its flesh wounded and
but one eye remarking sadly
the quick feet of passing men

they flavour their tea with shiba
mint leaves, rough sugar in lumps,
and take it with almond cakes

nothing in their medinas offends

yet each night someone pours smoking
dreams into my ears and nostrils

when my mouth opens
only arabic scribbles emerge

who turns my folded thoughts
back and forth   like
the pages of an unreliable book?

Oscar Wilde

my warden **stares   counting** again
clenched anxieties
                              worn
arguments crumbling reassurances
I've stolen from my day's ration

he looks oddly at the rose-red city
ruined inside my head
                              he measures
gaps opened by earthquakes in my skull

later he will prod at pigs
turn over one by one dazed hungers
squirming desires

would you now say to my people
the poems were worth it?

take these coins for my children
and say after
                    it was art I cared for
and despised life

Ark Poem

every night my body
floats light figures

boat-like they rise
the hierophants

their red sexual fingers

their cold questions
about Blake's Four Zoas
about the return
to orthography

unbearable angels
when they rise
I wake to thoughts
of deep water
                    sinkings

Canto

what I was promised I have not seen
no man in the stars no fiery brand
once an old woman ugly and tedious
as night limping beside a gate
prayerful couples nibbling words

the synagogue worm-eaten
grasshoppers flying
sky shaking with their glitter

I have nothing to hide
                   if it were
true I would say so the words
the preacher spoke rattle in my ears
like dried kernels
like grain shaking in dry fields

fields burn and are not burned

Ezra says:
             sunset
                  and the grasshopper flying

Saskatchewan Surveyor

at a correction line
he reads the wind's grammar

rhetoric falls from trees

in a simple sentence of land
a disappointed syntax

Argonauts, the CNE, etc.

with Herb on Saturday high on
grandstand and over roller
coaster still frame of lake
and tower coal barge begins
field force metre and rhyme as
downfield run or diagram

double blue abstract hits
striped abstract hits large
striped abstract falls and
scores:
           females hug their
wands
           saturday poem continues
next line downfield where
balls kicked
                     wan bruised
limps to an end
                     removes
larger than self a
hip thigh shoulder glob
ular head and
                     diminish
as lights go out here
and in every green field
force   poem ends
                     traffic

The Dogs of Nerja

and the neurotic dogs
and the dog star
and the wheels in the sky

the prophet: his head turned
his beard streaming like the stream
stars make in multiple exposures
and from his mouth
                    a balloon
and the words engraved

multiple man
                how much agony can you endure
                would you say
                does it really matter
                that sage renews itself
                that thyme becomes green once more

                and almond trees blossom

Samson

killing

again

he said he thought it was God
but remembered his father
the old quarrel
                law
the dark family
                    for that
collosal
        became monstrous

thus god   thus vision
thus in starlight
figure of a lion

sweet astrology

In Memory of Albert Camus

Camus: a headlight
in his chest broken
abstract tree

the road's focus
the road's intent
the road's abstraction
Camus: a road

in Saskatchewan, animal
blood
    slain cattle
      flung in pits
by Lumsden in a valley
roads leading to cattle pits
where slain cattle lie
miles from the beach
its bank and shoal
white with abstract tree

galaxy-city-beach
turning turning
        over a road
        where Albert Camus lies
        a headlamp in his eye

between the dagger
and the disease
between the dagger
and the stars

        desert: stumps
        of blind men (headlights
        in their eyes)
           know
        flowering daughters, know
        rose-flesh cactus girls

love
    heroism   says Camus

For Ann: On the Question of Franco's Successor

above me three ochre terraces
olive trees design another cliff
amid concrete, wood, new apartments
workmen sing flamenco casual
passionate
                    ochre land
                              red
land   slate mountains
yellow birds   day
sky   yellow as a finch
moon   looks
at a whitewashed house on a hill

is a great leap forward necessary
are fortunes to be made at a red bridge

we have felt our own colour, skin
in sun morning and moon night and

satisfied (we say) we see
land   sea

knowledge no longer a burden

we know freedom
                    songs

Locality

new year's eve my friend from Utah
remarks a cubist view of our village
from his apartment
                              church
pine tree
                    white tilted homes

"**our** village" I said

it was the need for art
made me greedy about lives
knowing nothing of their homes
or for that matter
                         our own

but it was cold
and our children made loud noise
driving out even these desperate spirits

late alone I remembered
it was not Spain but Estevan,
that home, I meant

Angelo's Wall

look: social justice is distraction
it comes out unequal with or without
evil men systematic changes order
disorder though you would have me declare
myself for or against good
                              here the sea is
blue the roof tiles orange the walls white
two workmen, one young, ruddy with beer I'd
say the other never quite able to straighten up
argue the consistency of mortar the curve
an arch should make over my Italian-American
neighbour's pseudo-Moorish wall
                              clouds move
against the mountain wall three   helicopters
turn (toward Algeciras?) these two
continue amiable intricate talk

as if this nation had no other history
and over there, war planes were not busy
with usual and unusual kinds of murder

Narrative Poem

the point is
the story
        that
one no one
        told

53

and yet
        cattle
on lean flanked
land leaning
toward plain

and yet
        shacks
coal fire
despair
        the
barbed wire
wolf willow
river ice

but never
a third act
plotting

end or
even

beginning

land
and long
land
        and
land

Earthworms Eat Earthworms
and Learn

as with Aunt Adeline
the one with the large bosom
one of the complicated cousins
who on a hot Regina afternoon
wept at a hurt finger
and thrust into her vagina
other fingers

so eating one another worm
knows inside another worm
the square root Adeline knew
and cousins knowing cousins
uncles uncles
aunts aunts

it goes on
wisdom of cells

this rod dividing into that
rod into that code that code

so it was with Aunt Eda
who coded Uncle Lou
who had himself been coded

into

and father knew father
mothering the last of the jews
who on the Hirsch land
put in new seed
and new codes
and new aunts

 so we survived
but had become
being as
we were

solutions

the seed

the new seed

final solution

remember forever the neon
Orpheum(?) Winnipeg 1935
lights exploding liquid
oh the elegant lobby
uncles and lights lights lights
then
        film

Agatha Christie

being civil she saw poison
as a flaw in character
and the use of a knife
a case history in Freud

difficult to explain
her dislike of jews

or why night upon night
she plotted solutions
to deaths she must have dreamed

her 200,000,000 readers
how much longing for murder
the neatness of England
is and still remains

though in Belfast, say,
bombs have other reasons
and no one explains

Message from Saturn

I have not forgotten
their camps   ovens
electronic dentists curators
surgeons newspapers genital
prongs   their devices

now the unmemory
the forgetting

knowing this witness
no other testimony

see they approach
children not knowing

how the planet burned
and from what star strangers came
their eyes their helmets
mask of turtle

children my children
welcome them
sing war songs old songs

Chief Dan Kennedy

when he was eighty
anthropology
impressed him
also memory

now at one hundred
he remembers
his dark wife
her silence

night night
what reason
what delight
either bed
or waking
could excuse

and down there
yes there the same
village whores
his people ours

he showed me
past
     English journals
with maps
pictures of Indians

On the Death of Ho Chi Minh

toward the end
he became frail as rice paper
his beard whispering thin ideograms

how unlike the great carved storm
that was Marx's face
                          how unlike
the darkness and fury
in Beethoven's head
                          scarcely
anything to be consumed

bombs destroy   destroy
you cannot touch his body now
or burn his poems

For Elie Weisel

bear witness: live it all
again content though source
be pitch and sewer
                          boneyard
skull place   golgotha

but what if jew
is only the german's
bad dream
                  you
pace through camps
at the world's end
beyond the horizon's barbed wire
close to the sun
                          endless oven

First Political Speech

first, in the first place, to begin with, secondly,
in the second place, lastly

again, also, in the next place, once more, moreover,
furthermore, likewise, besides, similarly, for example,
for instance, another

then, nevertheless, still, however, at the same time,
yet, in spite of that, on the other hand, on the contrary

certainly, surely, doubtless, indeed, perhaps, possibly,
probably, anyway, in all probability, in all likelihood,
at all events, in any case

therefore, consequently, accordingly, thus, as a result,
in consequence of this, as might be expected

the foregoing, the preceding, as previously mentioned

as already stated

Transition Table
from **Learning to Write** by Ernest
H. Winter (Second Revised Edition)
Macmillan (Toronto, 1961), p.156

Insomniac

They say Stalin at night
sleepless in the suburbs of Moscow
drew up long lists of enemies

think of that dreadful paper

65

to be sentenced by the pen
of an insomniac sleep-writing

new stars wheel over Spain
bulldozers cut roads through groves
in Africa moors rule who once ruled Spain

sleepless I pace before barred windows
fake-andalusian arches and toward sea
a Parador only cuts lines against the dark
where dark Greeks and Phoenicians sailed

if it is love that fingers in the mind
wake with a touch
                    curious
I remember only what was lost
plotting my own purges and despairs

On the 25th Anniversary of the Liberation of Auschwitz:
Memorial Services, Toronto, January 25, 1970
YMHA Bloor & Spadina

the name is hard
a German sound made out of
the gut guttural throat
y scream yell ing open
voice mouth growl
                        and sweat
"the only way out of Auschwitz
is through the chimneys"
                        of course
that's second hand   that's told
again Sigmund Sherwood (Sobolewski)
twisting himself into that sentence
before us on the platform
                        the poem
shaping itself late in the after
noon later than it would be:

Pendericki's "Wrath of God"
moaning electronic Polish theatric
the screen silent
                    framed by the name
looking away from /pretending not there
no name no not name no

        Auschwitz
    in GOTHIC lettering
                        the hall
a parody a reminiscence a nasty memory
the Orpheum in Estevan before Buck Jones
the Capitol in Regina before Tom Mix
waiting for the guns
waiting for the cowboy killers
one two three
                Legionnaires
Polish ex-prisoners Association
Legions
        their medals their flags

so the procession, the poem gradual
ly insistent beginning to shape itself
with the others

                    walked with them
into the YMHA Bloor & Spadina
thinking apocalypse shame degradation
thinking bones and bodies melting
thickening thinning melting bones and bodies
thinking not mine / must speak clearly
the poet's **words / Yevtyshenko at Baba-Yar**

there this January snow
heavy wet the wind heavy wet
the street grey white slush melted concrete
bones and bodies melting slush
                                        saw
with the others
                    the prisoner
in the YMHA hall Bloor & Spadina
arms wax stiff body stiff unnatural
coloured face blank eyes
                              walked
with the others toward the screen
toward the picture
                    SLIDES
            this is mother
            this is father
            this is
                    the one who is
waving her arms like that
is the one who
                    like
l mean running with her breasts bound
ing
        running
                    with her hands here and there
with her here and

                              there
          hands
                    that   that is
68   the poem becoming the body
          becoming the faint hunger
          ing body
                         prowling
                              through
          words the words words the words
          opening   mouths ovens
          the generals smiling saluting
          in their mythic uniforms god-like
          generals uniforms with the black leather
          with the straps and the intricate leather
          the phylacteries and the prayer shawl
          corsets and the boots and the leather straps

          and the shining faces of the generals in their boots
          and their stiff wax bodies their unnatural faces
          and their blank eyes and their hands their stiff hands
          and the generals in their straps and wax and stiff
          staying standing
                         melting bodies and thickening
                         quick flesh on flesh handling
                         hands

            the poem flickers, fades
        the four Yarzeit candles guttering one
            each four million lights dim
69   my words drift
                        smoke from chimneys and ovens
            a bad picture, the power failing
        pianist clattering on and over and through
    the long Saturday afternoon in the Orpheum
            while the whitehatted star spangled cowboys
                shot the dark men and shot the dark men
                and we threw popcorn balls and grabbed
                each other and cheered:
                                me jewboy yelling
    for the shot town and the falling men
                and the lights come on
                                and
                with the others
    standing in silence

    the gothic word hangs
    over us on a shroud-white screen

    and we drift away
                to ourselves
                    to the late Sunday Times
                        the wet snow
                        the city

                    a body melting

Sea Things

I

out of beige out of
darkness clamped on
its own completion

intestinal tail
shrimp
   thin
darkness of

worm
  shell and
cockle
   pink tongue
extruding of conch

in water
    outside
their bones
ours inside
pink
  extrusions

it is
  beauty always
of those I love
I admire

2

at Emma Lake
there was

71   John Cage
              lost

or so he said

and you are

in Spain

at least
           that is

your own

       story

Political Speech
  (for **PET**)

think: planets turn
        moons come into phase and out again
        tiny spanish birds rise to their own songs
        night comes and goes
        in the heavens constellations wheel
        and this man speaks

                        (beyond form
                            words like gyres
                            like Kubrick's great globe
                            its weltschmerz

        voices   voices

        at night they come to me
        disguised as clowns
        or in their sinister form
        as policemen, sisters
        asking me again
        to plunge down
        a great elevator
        to take a merry-go-round
        whose legs are silk pants

                            a sewer in my throat

but there are no voices
inside or outside this poem
neither a poem nor an opera
you said
        we're losing this now
it no longer makes sense
it isn't going to work

thesis: freedom
antithesis: necessity

if the revolution was about to occur
would the people of quebec rise up

the people of quebec would rise up

therefore the revolution was about to occur

wrong again
it goes another way:
                        since
you always did as I said
                        washed
your speeches wiped your rhetoric
clean as the parsing in your prose
looked after the creases in your biology
and the intertrigo in your quadrivium
you drew the following circles in the air:

            the nation is rational

                        (wrong)

            america is either good or bad

                        (equally wrong)

            canada is either possible or not

                        (still wrong)

and the possibility?

            only that we are older
            and awake
                        or not

Goya

I

the episode at Trueba: waiting
till clouds cleared so that
he could better see corpses

but what light could have shown
the real madness in that god
swallowing his own child?

ah, gay dancers of Madrid
bowing and posturing before
an endless blue canvas: cloud
tapestry-people did you know
he created you
               and these monsters?

"the episode at Trueba" from Goya's painting "may 3rd in Madrid The firing squad in La Moncloa":

75

Isidro, Goya's servant, tells of the night of the fusillades:

"From that same window my master watched the fusillades with a telescope in his right hand a small-mouthed blunderbuss with a handful of bullets in the left hand. If the French arrive here, my master and I are other Daoizes and Valardes. About twelve noon master said: 'Isidro, bring your blunderbuss and come with me' I obeyed him and where do you think we went? Well, we went to the Principe Pio Mountain, where the unburied bodies laid. I remember everything as if it had happened yesterday. It was a moonlight night, but the sky was full of menacing black clouds, one second it was clear, the next dark. My hair stood on end when I saw my master with the blunderbuss in one hand and his notebook in the other guiding me toward the dead bodies. As if he was worried he asked me: 'Are you trembling, Othello?' I, instead of answering him 'I'm trembling like a fennel' I almost began to cry, believing my poor master had lost his senses, because he called me 'Othello' instead of Isidro. Later we sat down on the river bank, near the dead bodies and my master opened his notebook, placing it upon his knees and awaited the moonlight which was temporarily hidden by a large cloud. Something hovered over the river bank grumbling and panting. Me, well, I trembled like quicksilver; but my master tranquilly continued as if it were daytime preparing his pencil and sketch. Finally, the moon shone as if it were daylight. In the middle of the puddles of blood we saw a group of cadavers some open-mouthed others head down, some as if they were kissing the ground, others with their hands bound...."

From **A New Complete Guide to the Prado Gallery** translated by Patricia May O'Neill, new edition revised by Myra Finkleman (Editorial Myfe, S.A. Madrid, 1966), pp.182-83.

The President and the Chairman Meet

I

when great men greet each other
with tea and wine and ceremony
small ones draw close
to guard themselves

2

there will be storms
as ever nightfall only
much later moon rising

3

drunkenness, prison, disgrace
a bad book of poems
                    who distinguishes?

two hundred years old the olive trees
twist under time no worse than ours

4

so many deeds cry out to be done
only the hour waits
                    and the chairman
and the congress   senators
before our great leap forward
before we find again the same
almond trees and the same moon

On the Cultural Revolution
(**for my university**)

our wheat fields almost empty
have we mined deeply enough
coal iron sulphur

77

but if you would not stoop
work with giant pines
there amid falling trees
think of the Restoration

what articles you might produce
you could clothe a nation

all things written on water
we cannot read the ancient script

Red Guards
(after Jean Luc Goddard)

1

ah! La Chinoise
you are burning Paris
yet you know nothing
of literature
            only
Quotations from Mao

comics

2

your head is a bomb
blue dynamite in your hands
your hair a black flag

your pardon   to
me you mentioned dialectic
noticed how bodies flew
out of wrecked automobiles

is that a theory of social change
or simply the love of man
and a woman

3

on barricades
cobblestones tear themselves from streets
assaulting policemen
the last industrialists still at work

before the indifferent screen
diminishes even their bulging eyes
I turn back to my work
but observing the icepick in your hand
write rapidly these pages on revolution

The President Speaks to the Nation

this is a poem called I have a plan

I heard the President say
                              his plan
plainly he said his plan

it was plain   because

he bent his mighty dark brows down
and quick as a helicopter flicking grass
out and away to fly to the wounded
licked upward his mighty lips

and said
          but

please excuse my saying anything
I ought not to say although
I want to tell you about plans

I have plans for
model cities miniature
poems like eggshell or china

that would ring true

he said the President said
he would not kill anyone
anymore and the way he would not kill

would be to let the killers kill
and then he would not be a killer

I think he said his plan
he had made out of models and secret
letters to old orientals
                         who

each night he cut up with his scissors
to paste on his eyelids

so that when we sang
when we sang
to that dead poet
who once wrote a poem about
the freedom of leg-irons
the President
                and this was
and he planned this

could smile
                and
the President could say

ah my loving people
we will work in the rice fields
and we will rebuild our roads
and we will climb together out
into the light unshaken mountains
where together
and this is my plan my people
we will kill americans

                please excuse my saying
                this poem

                I no longer like poetry

but when my eyes close
small poems like eggshells
drift in a white rice storm
past dead faces dreaming eyes

Political Science
(after Brecht and Trudeau)

in the cartoon by Groz
lechery   greed
                    those
outlines: spiritual beings

and here   the same vomit
chips lager iconic tits

there's your new nation
one   juridical
                    and free

Room XV

If you walk into Room XV of the Prado in Madrid you will see there
the most marvellous painting in the world. The painter, Velasquez,
stands at his easel, a delightful blonde princess, accompanied by her
maids in waiting, stands to his left and in front of him, to her left a
dwarf lady and a dog, behind them other attendants, and at the back
of the room, past a mirror that reflects two who are looking toward
the painter, an official opens a door to allow more light to enter. Look
closely and you will see that the spectators in the room XV are so life-
like that at first you do not notice the layers of pigment making up
their faces, the extraordinary application of paint to limb and cloth,
the cunningly calculated placing and perspectives, the miraculous
creation of even the atmosphere. So splendid is the illusion that you
could easily believe these figures walk, talk amongst themselves, and
go from room to room in the great museum to be admired by other
paintings, as the Maids of Honour admire us.

Cabinet Secrets

I

privy to secrets I'm giving this one
away free: Canadian Daniel Ellsberg
with 47 volumes of our own genuine Pentagon Papers
(secretly I've yearned to be an anarchist
enemy of the state, traitor, political prisoner
Clifford Irving
               at night I dream of
half-naked girls running through streets,
Stratford, Estevan, Yellow Grass, Corrinne)

I know the senior civil servant
who at 4:00 am in cold October
carried to the Governor General who
I think had not yet run his usual three
miles before breakfast the war measures
act to be signed
              once he showed me
the cabinet room the table where
ministers sit where the prime minister
sits where the civil servant sits at
a secretary's table of eighteenth-century
but it is especially maple or walnut or
curved and I know where he must have written
war measures

84

so it has been always
archangels with great golden eyes
you cannot look at   those aloof hands
those golden tables
                    listen: I have heard
they do secret studies they have profiles
so finally I think angels come to a hole
in the ground inside a house inside a farm

with aloof hands
they make coffins
photographs

and take the guns of revelation

terror dug out of the ground
like wet mice
                disappears
in the eternal silence

the cabinet

From "The Pentagon Papers"

Glossary:

AA	CAT	DIA	EPTEL (Deptel / Septel?)

AA   CAT   DIA
AAA   CHICOM   DOD
AID   CHINAT   FAL
ASA   CHMAAG   FAR
ABM   CIAP   FEC
AMB   CINCPAC   FMWA
ASAP COMUSMACV   FY
                                    FYI
                  LOC   MAAG   PACON
ICA   MAC   POLAD
ICC   KIA   MAP
I   MDAP   QTE
IDA
ISA

ROK RSM RSSZ RTA RVNAF RVNA   SAC SAM SAR
SMMSNIESTCSVNTAORTERMTETTFTO&ETRIMUNO
USAFUSGUSIAUSIBUSISUSOMUWVCVMVNVNAFVOA
WTYT
        UNQTE
            ROLLING THUNDER

            BARREL ROLL

BLUE SPRINGS FARMGATE FLAMING DART LEAPING LENA

The Trilemma:
        a. Will-breaking strikes on the North (para 7) are
        balked by (1) flash-point limits, (2) by doubts
        that DRV will cave and (3) by doubts that VC will
        obey caving DRV
        b. Large U.S. troop deployments. (para 9) are blocked
        by "French-defeat" and "Korea" syndromes, and Quat is
        queasy. (Troops could be net negatives, and be beseiged).
        c. Exit by negotiations (para 9) is tainted by the
        humilation likely to follow.

insurrection defection dissension impotence defeatism concession
accommodation

86   risks:

deployment of Frogs and Sams in North Vietnam
hot pursuit flak suppression strike strikes strikes

losses panic revulsion sympathetic fires over
Berlin, Cyprus, Kashmir, Jordan waters

stretch-out retard the program
circuit breaker

shunt

On the Renewal of Bombing
in VietNam December, 1972

At **the sight** of this photograph
forming itself out of headlines and print
what should a poet do but cry out
that the dead are no less real
for falling into pictures of ruined cities

I do not mean to speak as a prophet
that cherished tone now detached
as if voice itself could be flung into space
without body
    At my kitchen table
The Toronto Star lies beside tall salt cellars
and where Bess Truman stares
with her closed gaze
     Nadezhda Mandelstam's
Hope Against Hope, I notice, wears its purple
cover like a funeral robe.

Tonight in our cities no doubt some
one will cry out
     my daughter
sees in her dark room nameless horrors
and like photographs
      silent and distant
the dead will fall
     in the sum of
all days, nights, deaths, stars,
I hear this poem like a disembodied voice
less powerful than even a composition
made out of lead type and black ink

Ottawa October 70

winter the gatineau winter snow
Mike Snow's film and from the Skyline
roads curl like snow blind wind
drift
        and the river curls in its iron
turning
            iron flowers in a wind
        over the city
                        city winds
grey-blue iron white grey

film
    in the Cabinet glows
grey night   late fire

        law

Mike Snow's film in the National
Art Centre
                back and forth
                back and forth
                back and forth
child
                back and forth
                back and forth
window
        back
                teacher
                        forth
we
    there are
                law

are in
winter again
child's time
            the law
the iron   law
holds us as iron holds tongues
as iron holds ice as iron is
iron law we have come again to
iron-time
            the return
                        our words
visible as a snow a time of
                        it is
again
        the prison of dream of
        prison

                        words words words the words

                        law
again
        winter

                        and snow closes over
                        ottawa   grey city
                        the city
                                a book closing
                        a closed white book

Nerja

I

that ship
or
   is it
on the horizon

90

so: perception

you are close
to me you are

there
      it is
the horizon

holds there
three
        diminishing
ships

2

if you are there

say so

91

to me

    from hills

from ochre cities

from the ill-clad

speak

    words of

    the tower

its presence

      at least

3

this poem is built to
see through

92   see through

this poem

                see

through

              it

is

   nothing

                nothing

is this poem see

through

              over and
over   I said
nothing
              no one
believed
              me

or the poem
                  not

there

        see

The Garden of Delights

and so we went down to the river
to the corpses there but on our way
beside a willow copse we heard ring-
ing sounds as if a tree were hung
with bells and looked to see the willow
blossom into crystal as if its leaves
were birds
         so from the branches hung
lovers copulate their loves dropping
into a giant pool where storks and emus
swam with copulating lovers in their wings
while from their eggs emerged the limbs
of love and lovers clasping legs about
crystal goblets, bells and some stroked
flutes that blew sweet music from their
assholes while others sucked the tongues
of birds being fucked by mice or toads
or long-eared sages whose bald heads
served service to young balding girls
their legs entwined about the sage's eyes
and all went circling round the pool
of love
    now
        two such bodies will
not be seen again
          love dear
in them life dear in them

so I looked at corpses, noticing
three female death still coy in them
and thought the whole world is a coffin
and a bed
       and watched the river wash
blood over a dark city near the top
(or bottom) left of Bosch's tryptich

Velasquez: Las Meninas

change the lines about
stone man and stone moon
to read   reflect on images

94

(fish locked in ice
like a memory of summer)

since form longs to be free
and not to know its name

just so
        Velasquez put him-
self into **Las Meninas** creat-
ing not only "a theology
of painting"
                but self:

(if he is
        there who
painted the picture?

Gautier: "but where is the
picture?")
                neither anecdot-
al nor deceitful
                measured

as if in that court your
life "saved" depended on

style: looking "as if"

so that Dona Margarita looks
out as deformed Maria Barbola
looks out
        at (being looked at
by The Maids in Waiting) Felipe?
Mariana? who look into a mirror
looking out at you looking at

them
        as if
                I hadn't saved the
poem from the moon stone

and the stone man

        2

if he is looking at the
picture he could not have
painted it
                if he isn't
how could he have painted
it
  if he painted it
where was he
                        if he is
in it

        3

"We observe the artist is
not painting on the canvas
which we as spectators are
viewing"
                Complete Guide
                to the Prado etc.

        4

reflect: if he is
not painting **that**
painting

        5

"calculating the real
existence of atmosphere"

Envoi

my country is not a country
                                but winter

rivers of ice
from St. Hubert terrible knives
run through the whiteness of my veins

politics pierce my heart
on a floor littered with history
I shiver while wardens shovel in
lunatic sentences, rag upon rag

it must be cold in prison, in québec

and your heart hurt singer
what do you see through its pane

icy slaves circle the river
montréal tense against the steel of its manacles
your words drifting like frozen wounds
                                blessing
a sick bride
a murderous bridegroom
                        that wedding
whose children will be colder killers
than the words of this or any other song

Eli Mandel was born in Estevan, Saskatchewan, of Russian-Jewish immigrant parents. He studied at the Universities of Saskatchewan and Toronto after service as a medical corpsman in World War II. He has taught at the Royal Military College at St. Jean, Quebec, and at the University of Alberta. Now a Professor of Humanities and English at York University, he is known not only as a poet but as a critic and editor.

An **Idiot Joy** received the Governor General's Award for poetry in 1967. His selected poems **Crusoe** is his most recent publication.

Some of the poems in **Stoney Plain** have appeared elsewhere in slightly different versions. "Auschwitz", in particular, has been completely revised for this book.

The buffalo motif is from a sixteenth century European sketch based on accounts of early explorers to North America.

The design of this book has been prepared in collaboration with the author.

Text set in 9.5 Century on Compugraphic phototypesetting equipment by Alive Press (Guelph). The paper is Byronic Text. Printed offset in March, 1973 on a Multi 1250. Binding by Universal Book Bindery (Toronto).

Printed in Canada on Canadian paper.